Copyright © 2024 by Pippa Bird

All rights reserved. No part of this book may be reproduced or transmitted in any form or by any means, electronic or mechanical, including photocopying, recording, or by any information storage and retrieval system, without permission in writing from the publisher.

ISBN: 9781763833845

First Edition

Corroborate Cockatoo

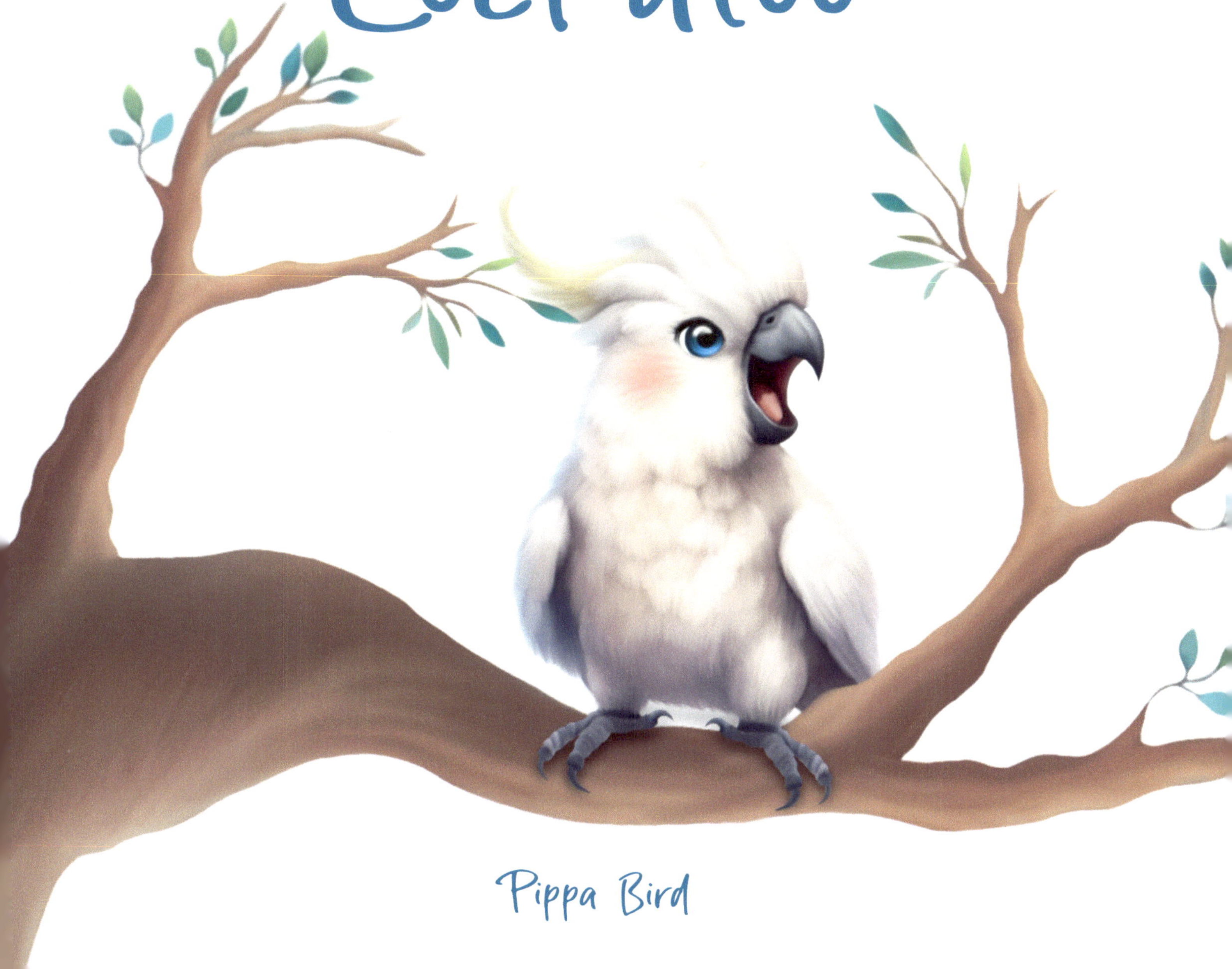

Pippa Bird

In the heart of the Aussie bush, where laughter was true,
Lived Clancy Cockatoo with a great point of view.

One sunny day, under a big gum tree,
Clancy gathered his friends

'Come and sit with me!'

"Hey pals," said Clancy, with a flap and a wink,
"Let's talk about feelings, it's
easier than you think!"

"When Quincy feels sad and just wants to cry, We corroborate his feelings—show we get why."

Warren crawled up, with ears all perked,
"How do we prove it's real, not some big quirk?"

Clancy nodded, feathers all neat,
"To substantiate feelings, we just take a seat."

"Squawk. Substantiate. Cockatoo. Cockatoo. Substantiate. Cockatoo-oo."

"We listen and care, and give them some room,
For in showing we understand, friendships can bloom.

"If Frank feels grumpy and starts to berate,
We validate his feelings; it's never too late."

"By echoing their thoughts, and doing our bit."

Emma then giggled, "How do we show it's legit?"

"We authenticate feelings, make sure they're heard,
A simple act of kindness, without saying a word."

With a cheer and a chirp, Clancy Cockatoo wrapped it up, "Validating feelings fills every friendship cup."

"In our lovely bush home, where our bonds are bright,
We support one another, every day and every night."

So, in the bushland where animals roam free,
They learned from Clancy Cockatoo, beneath that big tree.

With hearts full of laughter, understanding, and cheer,
They validated feelings, year after year.

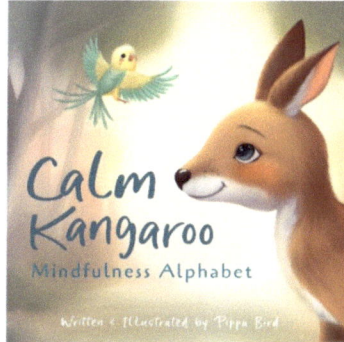 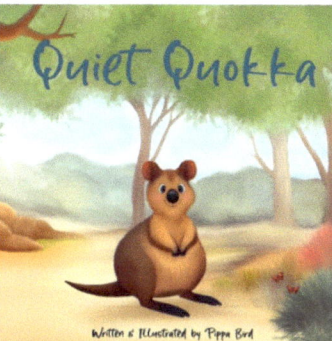  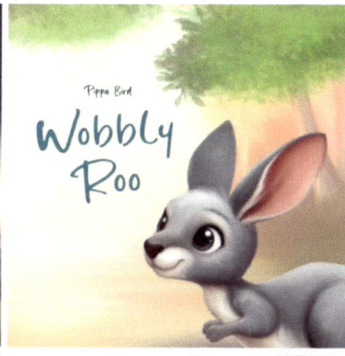
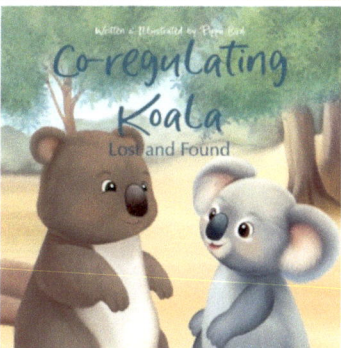 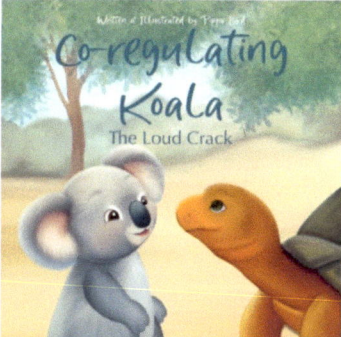 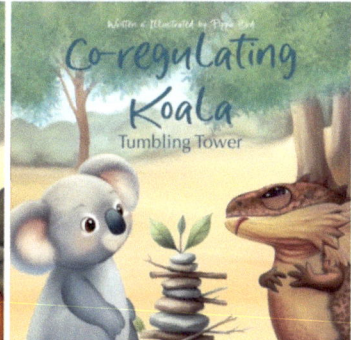 
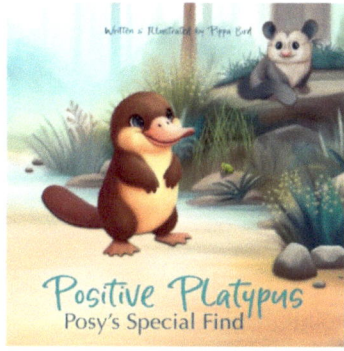 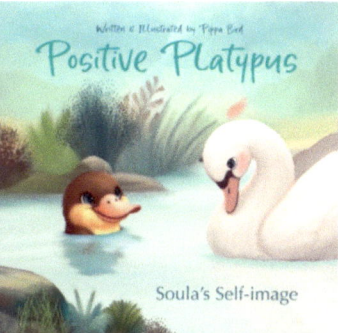

Calm Kangaroo

Introducing Calm Kangaroo's Mindfulness & Wellbeing Journal: 10 Week Program

Designed to enhance emotional learning and mental wellbeing. This delightful adventure invites children to explore mindfulness and self-care with weekly wellbeing check-ins and self-reflections, mindfulness colouring and expressive art activities. Available now on Amazon!

70+ Full-colour pages

www.ingramcontent.com/pod-product-compliance
Lightning Source LLC
Chambersburg PA
CBHW041544040426
42446CB00003B/228